Always the UNCHOSEN

All those unsaid feelings

AMINA SARTAJ

First Edition
Published by Amina Sartaj

ISBN: 9798312615531
Cover Design: Amina Sartaj
Interior Design: Amina Sartaj

Introduction

The book, Always the Unchosen, is a collection of broken poetry that speaks to those who feel unseen, unheard, and burdened by silent pain. It's for the ones who smile despite their wounds, the ones who carry their heartbreak quietly, and the ones who have felt like an afterthought in their own stories.

The poetry within captures the raw emotions of being unnoticed, unchosen, and unseen, yet it also serves as a comfort—a place where you can find your own unspoken feelings reflected in words. Each poem is a whisper to the soul, a quiet acknowledgment of the struggles people often hide beneath the surface.

The book isn't just about sadness—it's about recognition and understanding. It gives voice to emotions that are difficult to express, making readers feel less alone in their pain. Whether it's about lost love, self-doubt, or simply the longing to be understood, Always the Unchosen acts as a companion for those who need to hear: I see you. I feel you. You are not alone.

This book belongs to you now. Let it speak to the wounds you never show.

For, the broken version of you that only exists when you are all alone.

To the reader's,
You have been through things you never said about,
I'm sorry if this book makes you cry, but it's okay to cry,
it's a process of healing and I want you to heal.
You have gone through alot on your own.
Only you know the days of tolerating heartbreaks,
Stroms , sorrows, agony on your own.
And i wish you thank yourself,
for never giving up on yourself.

Always the unchosen

And you heard them because you knew
how it feels to be unheard,
You loved them because you knew how
it feels to be unloved,
You did it all because you never wanted
them to experience those things you
went through
You were always the healer but never
the healed.

Always the unchosen

A glass which is already cracked can be
broken by a touch,
In the same way,
The heart which is cracked can be broken
by a word.

Always the unchosen

And sometimes your heart is filled with words
that reflect the pain of unspoken emotions,
The weight of heartbreak,
The beauty found in sadness,
The warmth flowed in tears.

Always the unchosen

May you find someone who doesn't care about their ego when it comes to you,
May you find someone who can try their best to make up your mind,
May you find someone who loves you when they are busy not only when they are free,
May you find someone who makes you feel important when you feel you aren't worth anything,
May you find someone who accept all your flaws forgive all your mistake,
May you find someone who prefer losing anything rather than losing you,
May you find someone who stand with you when you're at your lowest,
May you find someone who stays forever.

Always the unchosen

The world is too big
but, *lil for me*
The people are so many
but, *none for me*

Little things that aren't little

- text me when you reach home
- did you have dinner on time?
- you seem upset..is everything alright?
- makes efforts to fix my mood
- remembering small details
- can catch every slight change in my behaviour
- gets mad if I accidentally hurt my self
- even if we are arguing never raises his voice
- never gives up on me even after tons of fight
- gets my favourite snacks/chocolates without even asking for it.

Always the unchosen

I was unbroken before -
Before, the wind stole my bliss
Before, the night took my peace
Before, my love broke my heart

Always the unchosen

You think of them,
before you think of you.
You always kept them,
before your own self.
In the end.
still you were the one,
left out alone.

Always the unchosen

Didn't i deserve to be loved? Didn't i deserve to be known? Didn't i deserve to be heard? Didn't i deserve to be cared? Didn't i deserve to be internally happy? Didn't i deserve everything i would love to do for others?

Always the unchosen

And you chose to hide it in your heart,
The blade like words,
Sharp as knife,
Made you bleed from in and out,
Still you chose to hide it in your heart.

Always the unchosen

And I lost a piece of myself,
Which was named as
peace.

Always the unchosen

It's hard to let go someone you love with all your heart,
Sometimes we hold too tightly expecting that
everything must end with peace and bliss,
But not every conversation needs closure,
Not every relationship needs a perfect goodbye,
Not every dreams meant to have meanings,
There should be a insight in understanding.
Some things serve their purpose even in
incompleteness,
just like a half written poem, still holds the pain.

Always the unchosen

A thing which Is broken can be fixed for once
But,
A thing which is broken again and again is of no use.

what about your heart?

Always the unchosen

Only if you knew the pain of leaving is
equal to being left.
I know being left is painful, but leaving
someone you love more than your own
self is excruciating, you'll forever be
guilty to break their heart even though
you broke you heart too-
There comes a time in your life you'll
never be able to accept anyone or love
anyone because the person you left
didn't leave your mind.

i hope you never get in a situation to
leave your love.

Always the unchosen

I gather pieces of my heart, But the bandage ain't stick anymore, Then the stranger secured my heart, Again then dropped my heart like glass.

Always the unchosen

And you know, what's the best thing about you?
The way little things makes you happy,
If you receive a flower from someone you immediately be the happiest person alive,
If someone writes you a letter tears of joy start to fall apart from your eyes,
You can't help to hide your emotions when someone remember's a small detail about you,
I wish you be the same today, tomorrow, forever.

Always the unchosen

Always the unchosen,
Always the unheard,
Never found the words to
Describe myself, my heart.

Always the unchosen

Sometimes it was hard for me to find words for what I
was experiencing, i didn't knew how to gather words
and frame it to tell them how it feels,
It's just blank-
No words in my mind, no answers for the question I've
been asked.
And then I read a quote that goes, **Cursed are those
who feel Oceans but can only express a drop.**
This made me feel like I'm not the only one.

thankyou, to whoever wrote this.

And,
i wonder will i ever be loved the way I imagined myself to be loved as.

Always the unchosen

The only difference was,
I tried my best not to break your heart,
You tried your best not to break their heart.

Always the unchosen

It would be much better if me/myself would
work on those advise I gave to others,
It would be much better to move on from
things that broke me apart,
It would be much better if I would have
prioritised myself.

Always the unchosen

The only launguage i could never be
fluent in,
no matter how hard I try is explaining
myself what I feel inside.

Always the unchosen

It was me who chose the knife,
when all i ever needed was bandage.

Always the unchosen

Was so in love that
I even lied to
myself about
every single thing
that broke me.

Always the unchosen

Even your little is alot to me,
Even your hii is a story to me,
Even your blink is a dream to me,
Even your smile is a world to me,
Even your hairs is perfume to me,
Even your little is a lot to me.

but the fact my everything is
nothing to you.

Always the unchosen

I was always the "wasn't good enough" sibling.

Always the unchosen

Everything i ever loved,
ever craved,
ever needed,
ever wanted for the rest of my life,
Left me.

Always the unchosen

And i wonder,
How broken I was,
When I begged for my own death
while I saw others begged to
save their lives.

Not everything you lose is a loss, sometimes losing something which is close to you might break your heart but later you'll get to know how lucky you were to lose that to find something you never dreamt of, something makes you feel like it's more than you deserve- So, when something or someone walks away, don’t always see it as a defeat. It might just be a way of clearing the path for something much better for you.

Paper listened to me more than *people* did.

Always the unchosen

I wish I knew how to cut off my expectations,
so that it couldn't hurt me again and again.

Always the unchosen

Would you still choose me when the one you
loved comes back to you?

some questions just never let me sleep.

Always the unchosen

I was always a "maybe" so I don't know how it feels to be chosen or what it feels to be chosen,
I was always a "backup plan" and "just in case"
I could work if the Main person couldn't, but i could never be the main person,
The only difference between me and her was, she was chosen by him and I was available for him.

Always the unchosen

With every word you bring
me peace,
your eyes just blinks *a*
thousand dreams.

Always the unchosen

Only if I knew how long it would take
to fix everything that's broken in me,
They say time heals everything,
But my time has been stopped since
the day you left.

Always the unchosen

I dreamt of a world,
where everything feels so right
where I can be loved right and hugged tight.

Always the unchosen

Just because you cry alot doesn't mean you aren't strong enough,
you cry because your heart is pure, you are just sensetive and being sensetive is not a flaw- it's a gift.
Sensetive people experience the world deeply,
You can't help if things break your heart too easily,
you can't help if the bitterness of words tear you apart easily.
Feeling too much is the point of having a heart,
a heart which is pure.
so next time if you feel to cry,
Cry.

Always the unchosen

There were days with endless pain,
There were times of unstoppable struggle,
You carried it all then and now,
The weight of taunts couldn't let you down,
And when the nights were cold and long
You heard the echoes of fierce and strong.

Always the unchosen

And then I realised I suffered more in
my imagination compared to reality and
the worst part among all of them is,
I keep on expecting things knowing it
will end up hurting me,
As always my own expectations were
the one to hurt me the most.

Always the unchosen

Heal yourself, the way you heal others.

Always the unchosen

You dreamt to be loved without measures,
and you found the love full of mournings.
You dreamt a life full of laughter and love,
and you found a life full of sorrows and goodbyes.

Always the unchosen

On days when you felt like you
couldn't breathe,
It was you who stood with yourself.
Only you knew what you've been
through, only you knew how hard it
was for you not to give up.

please give yourself credit for it.

Always the unchosen

I hate how effortlessly tears starts to escape from my eyes,
every single time I think of you leaving.

Always the unchosen

It was easy to say sorry, but it wasn't easy to
accept the sorry because,
Sentence written in sorrows and pain
Yet can't erase the bleeded stain.
A page filled with sorry - but still I see
The ink won't rewrite what you did to me.

Always the unchosen

World is full of stories, some find their happy ending and other remain half ended,
Abiding between what was and what could have been, we start to imagine happy endings to fit in the world and peacefully spend our remaining life,
But the fact is, not everyone is meant to be completed,
some stories are meant to stay unfinished.

Always the unchosen

And how could I move on,
If my favourite part of life were
moments spent with him.

Always the unchosen

I wish you made efforts to keep me,
I wish you did everything you ever said,
I wish you never asked me to leave,
A wish, just a wish.

Always the unchosen

Everything I was afraid to happen, happened
Everything i ever needed, left
Everything i loved, wasn't for me.

Always the unchosen

Where were you in the nights i cried til I can't breathe,
Where were you when I didn't even know what's wrong with me,
Where were you when my mind full of thoughts were attacking my heart,
Were were you when I needed someone to hold me tight,
Were were you when I needed to feel safe,
Were were you when I needed you the most.

Always the unchosen

Her tears carried the emotions countless,
The heaviness of a single drop is boundless.

What's love to you?
- a feeling of being safe

Always the unchosen

I knew, I knew it's going to end and my heart is going to break again,
I knew everything's going to be the same again.

Always the unchosen

I always needed someone to look things
from my point of view,
Someone to understand me without
explaining,
The one who could hear me in and out,
The one who can find the truth in my lies,
The one who sees the best in me at my
worst times.

Always the unchosen

Only if they knew, it's not my anger
it's my heart screaming that *i'm deeply hurt.*

Always the unchosen

I've gone through the worst,
to find the best
still couldn't make him mine.

Always the unchosen

Seeing those school girls laugh til it gets hard for them to
breathe, reminds me of us.
when homework was the only tension,
waking up in the morning was the only mission
and, carrying bags were the only burden.

i miss you - the teenage me.

Always the unchosen

They say everything is temporary,
yes it is.
but the pain it gives, is that temporary too?

Always the unchosen

Then they yelled at you, and you started crying,
not because of being yelled,
just because you've been holding things from so long and now that you are tired of being in the same situation from so long, your heart started to ache and you couldn't be able to hold your tears.

Always the unchosen

You broke me in a way,
nobody could heal.
or, maybe i never want to be healed
because *you broke me.*

Always the unchosen

And how fragile we are that we
couldn't control ourselves from
getting attached to stuffs that would
break us apart.
No matter how robust you are when it
comes to your heart (a heart which is
pure) you are nothing but fragile.

Always the unchosen

The boat swims until it's in water,
but when water gets in the boat, it's
drowned.
in the same way,
you love when you receive the same
love,
but if you love when and you keep on
recieving the pain
you know you are going to be
drowned.

Always the unchosen

I'll always hate the way it ended,
but the memories we made together are worth all the pain.

After all,
وہ عشق ہی کیا جو درد نہ دے۔

Always the unchosen

And i wrote you in a way, nobody could read you.

Always the unchosen

You said you love me, but you didn't mentioned you love to make me cry too.

Always the unchosen

Every time I come to you with a broken
heart and eyes full of tears, not because
I want you to do something for me, it's
just your presence heal the things what's
broken in me, the way your arms
wrapped around me comforts my soul,
i feel safe around you.

Always the unchosen

I hope she breaks your heart,
the way you broke mine.
i hope she leaves you at your lowest,
the way you left me.

Always the unchosen

Sometimes we all crave a break from the world,
from every unnecessary sufferings,
From everything which leads us to heartbreaks,
Give yourself the time your soul deserves.
After all those silent sufferings you've been,
you deserve peace, you deserve love.

Always the unchosen

You said you know me the best,
then why I've to pretend I'm okay with things
which are internally breaking me apart,
If only you knew me,
you would've known how bad it hurts.

Always the unchosen

Can't help with the heavy breaths when the flashbacks appear.

Always the unchosen

I wish it ended differently between you and me,
not in silence, not in pain, not in echoes of our
laughter fading in the air.
I wish we had a temporary goodbye ends when
you reach home after your business trip.
A goodbye in a gentle way,
not the way door slammed at my face.
A part of me will always wish,
it ended differently between you and me.

Always the unchosen

If only we had more time, to make memories a lifetime,
To feel your hands tuk my hair behind my ears,
To feel the deepness of love when I look at the moon and you look at me,
To see you admiring me every single time you look at me.
If only we had more time, just a little to make it forever.

Always the unchosen

The words i never said, I wish I would've said.
You are my moon, you are my star, you are
everything i admire from afar.
You are the thought stuck in my head,
You are the person stuck in my heart.
i wish I would've said, I love you before you left.

Always the unchosen

The version of us exist in my mind,
is a dream to be reality,
a wish to be fulfilled.

Always the unchosen

I wish I stayed a bit longer,
I wish I knew losing you'd be my worst choice,
I wish I knew I'm going to lose myself after losing you,
I wish I knew how to spend my life with your memories,
The thoughts of you are comforting me and breaking me at the same time,
i wish you knew I'm regretting after losing you.

Always the unchosen

How to heal pain of broken
promises?
Those which made me feel
grateful for once, those which
made me thank to God,
Just the promise, broke the
building of expectations,
just a promise, just a broken
promises

Always the unchosen

You moved on still I'm stuck in the cafe you
introduced me to the girl your mom chose for you,
Found your wedding card in my mailbox,
how easy it was for you to change the main person
from the plan we made for us.
Now, I heard god gifted you a baby girl, happy for the
sweet family but,
kinda funny, *you moved on and still I'm stuck in the*
cafe, you introduced me to the love of your life.

Always the unchosen

It's better to never be loved, rather than being loved and left quick.

Always the unchosen

I'm still waiting for the sorry you never said,
Everthing would be okay, only if you realised
Those words which are left unspoken,
Could've changed everything, I've been
waiting till today.

Always the unchosen

I wish I fought harder,
this time for myself.
To let go people,
who are okay to leave.

Always the unchosen

It could be people we spend
10years with and still find hard
to explain ourselves or,
It could be people we spend 10
days and don't even need
words to explain what we find
hard to say.

it's up to you.

Always the unchosen

The older you get the more you realise nobody ever kept you before themselves. "They were available for you when they had free time, but they never freed their time to be available for you."

Always the unchosen

Oh, to have a guy who never
writes about anything but when it
comes to me he owns a diary
which screams about me.
Oh, to be loved by the guy.

Always the unchosen

I don't know what kind of life I'm living in,
one side I'm giving advice to people every
thing is going to be fine,
on the other, I don't know what's going on
in my own life.

Always the unchosen

It feels like impossible to let go someone with
who you dreamt to spend your whole life,
Just the thought of letting go gives you
mentally yet physical pain too, your heart
aches as if someone kept a heavy rock on your
chest and it gets hard for you to breathe.
It makes you realise,
"*if the thought is affecting me this much I can't
imagine what's going to happen when you'll
actually leave*" and you keep on overthink
until the last moment you spend with them,
you can't even believe the things you
overthinked about is actually happening.

*you can't help but to accept the reality, that
they left.
they left, they were meant to leave.*

Always the unchosen

You are the same girl when you feel burden to express your feelings, The same kid who was named as "too much".

Always the unchosen

Someone out there dreams
to stay with you,
While,
you dream to stay with
those who break your heart.

Always the unchosen

I developed peace in me with the thought,
I can't have everything i wish for,
somethings should be awaited to make
me understand the worth of owning
things which only belongs to me. To make
me realise i should be grateful for things i
never thank about.

And i never had people to text, when I wanted to have a deep conversation about my situation.

Always the unchosen

There's a different type of calmness when you know the person you love isn't looking for someone else except you.
i wish to experience that too.

Always the unchosen

There comes a habit of giving people
too much-
that when it comes to you,
choosing yourself feels ilegal.

Always the unchosen

I'm the kind of person who'll listen your
excuses even after watching your actions
which showed the truth.
I know what you feel about me, it's just i
chose silence over unnecessary drama.

Always the unchosen

And I'll wait till the date you find me again,
Maybe my prayers will be answered.

Always the unchosen

Nobody prepares you for the misery life puts you in, You get broken and then learn to heal on your own, You get lost then learn to find yourself in darkness, Your thoughts get tangled then you learn to disentangle them. *as you grow, you learn to grow.*

Always the unchosen

And to explain what hurts you,
Is to experience it again,
To live in the moment again which left you shattered,
To watch them be so cold against you
to break you in pieces.
To feel the wind throwing Blade on you
when they mentioned you always meant nothing to them.
to feel the worst times of your life again.

Always the unchosen

She said,
She's in love with the moon while
having the whole galaxy in her eyes.

Always the unchosen

Let them think wrong about you,
Don't ruin yourself by the thought of them,
knowing the truth,
If they would've known you, they would know about you.
You can't clarify everyone about the real you.

Always the unchosen

He was a sun in winters and I was the cold ground,
I was warmed for a moment but left colder when
he was gone.

Always the unchosen

It just takes a second to remind
each moment spend with you.
just a second.
to re-watch my own love story
which was a sad ending.

Always the unchosen

The way my heart is
tied with the wire of
your thoughts,
tightening every time I
think of you leaving.

Always the unchosen

It's 3:00 am, You stare at the ceiling wondering it's been 4 hours laying, after trying your best still you weren't able to find sleep, You knew it requires a lot of struggle to free your head, to shut your mind. You didn't have enough peace to make you sleep.

Always the unchosen

You deserve to be the main lead
of the novels you read.

Always the unchosen

There is no guarantee the person you are
breathing for,
will be yours for sure.

Always the unchosen

I was always the one to admire the couples from afar, it makes me smile to see them loving each other, it makes my day to watch a guy feeding his woman from his hands, i wish the purity in them remains forever.

even though I'm not experiencing it, atleast they are, I'm happy for them because they make me happy.

Always the unchosen

I think the worst part about me is,
For some people, I'm always the
forgiving, the forgetting.
I'll keep on forgiving things no
matter how many times it breaks me,
the thought that this was a mistake
by them, they are sorry for it, it's
okay to forget and forgive, is stucked
in my head.
And then the loop never ends.

Always the unchosen

If you love them, show them.
make them feel loved , tell them they are the most important person for you, make them feel heard, express your feelings as much as you can. This is the best thing in relationship to make them feel extra special, to make them feel they are never going to be alone you'll always have their back.

Always the unchosen

The kind of love we all deserve,
"you get more gorgeous every time I look at you"

Always the unchosen

A letter to my past self,

The worst thing you ever asked God for— was to grow old as soon as possible. I wish you knew that the life you are living now is the best part of your life. One day, you will look back and realize that the moments you are living now will become your favorite memories – the ones you'll hold onto forever.

I wish I could tell you to live a little more because, as you grow older, everything that makes you happy will start to fade, one by one.

You are so strong, I love you.

~ Your adult self

Always the unchosen

I wish the word " I miss you" holds
I'll come back to you,
and the word " I love you " holds
I'll never leave.

Always the unchosen

We are scared to ask some questions
because we know the answers would break
us in a way it would be hard for us to heal.

Always the unchosen

You always had the loving side of me, the caring side of me, the always available side of me, the sacrificing side of me, you had the side which people barely find in me, but unfortunately you chose to lose it.

Always the unchosen

They say difficult roads leads you to beautiful destinations.

indeed I was on the difficult way where every
path i stepped was layered with spikes,
i bleeded on every roads , still the destination
i reached was worst than the journey.
still the destination i reached made me cry
even more harder.

Always the unchosen

There should be something
wrong with me,
If the whole world finds
hard to love me.

Always the unchosen

I searched the lost peace of me in every soul
which was close to me,
Lately, I realised it was in the depth of me.

Always the unchosen

I was a flower grown alone between the cracks,
Watching every other in the field together forever.
People admire them, click pictures with them, and
me I'm the one who comes in the middle of the way
to interrupt people, I'm the one who get stepped
on everytime they cross.
because I deserve it.

Always the unchosen

Even your favourite things
don't make you happy
anymore when they make
you feel like a burden.

Always the unchosen

I always had
to say
goodbye to
those who
felt like
home.

Always the unchosen

Learn to leave those people who always blame you for everything.

Always the unchosen

Even the moon goes to phases from losing everything to again be at the fullest, while being all alone.

Always the unchosen

And only if it was possible to disappear from the world when it hurts you a little too much without knowing the fact that you have no shoulder to lay your head on, no human to hold you down. It's just you to suffer, no one who is affected, or being hurt because you are suffering. It's just you, it was always you.

Always the unchosen

Maybe he was mine to lose and i was his to use.

Always the unchosen

Then they make you
feel regret, for being
extra caring to them,
they make you
question yourself
why were you too
good to them,
because the way you
were understanding
them is the way they
were using you.

Always the unchosen

There comes a time when
you start to fear people
and crave loneliness, you
hate when a group of
people get in your room,
you love your room being
empty as always, you find
peace in being solitary, you
start to avoid people
because there's no time for
you to get in the
unnecessary drama they
create, you love being you
in your room with your
favourite books and your
happy soul.

Always the unchosen

How to unlove the person your heart loves, when you know the person is not good for you, but your heart still chooses to stay, you know the person is going to break you, still your heart chooses to be broken. Only if you knew the way to ask your heart to obey you, because the world is ready to break it.

Always the unchosen

Not every past deserves to be remembered,
some memories are terrifying.

Always the unchosen

The way your heart
carries intense pain and
when asked about, still
chooses to say
"everything is fine".

Always the unchosen

It took me so long to understand, I was the
favourite umbrella until the summer arrived, I was
the peace every time you came from the trip you
craved to have me until you found your new home.
I was your childhood hoodie you chose to keep
with yourself forever even after turning old until
you found the new one.
Until you found the new love -

Always the unchosen

Everything was too
loud to be able to
hear the noise of
my breaking heart.

Always the unchosen

You've been the child grown up while learning to keep things inside you, you've always been the teenager who was never enough even though you gather all of your strength together to be perfect for them. You are the adult who learnt to live the life with the broken heart.

Always the unchosen

I don't care if no one notices any changes in me,
but I'm in need to be noticed by you.

Always the unchosen

And the nerve
you have to
blame me for
having scars
while you were
the one who
gifted me those.

Always the unchosen

I wish, while you were holding my hand you held a little tighter when you felt I was pulling away, instead of letting me leave.

What's the
point of
living the life
where you
aren't even
living.

Always the unchosen

But you never struggled for me, I've never seen anyone struggling for me, to solve my problem, to make things easy for me, to pull me out of days I'm stuck in, to travel in the metro even if it's too rushed just because I was craving the french toast you make. *Never -*

Always the unchosen

How strange, you spend all your day
thinking of them what they did? what
they had? are they okay?
but,

Let go - *some things are better unsaid.*

Always the unchosen

Ever wondered? how your
words can make a stranger
feel so special,
To be kept as one of their
favourite memories.

Always the unchosen

I don't want anything from you but
promise me you'll take care of yourself.

Just a sentence?
Not really -

Always the unchosen

Nothing really feels so fake like the smile you try to widen up after seeing them with someone else.

Always the unchosen

Have you ever been in a situation where they tell you they can't lose you but never even try to keep you, they say they'll call you at 12:00 PM and you just keep on checking your phone till 12:00 AM yet still no calls. You trust their words but their actions speak a different story.

Do more of
things that
makes you
happy,
because
yes.
Nobody
cares
about you.

Always the unchosen

You chose to replace me with her and I
chose to replace you with peace.
We're built differently.

No matter how
much you
broke me, I'm
never going to
pray for your
downfall.

Always the unchosen

You have the ocean of feelings in you,
But never express any,
Not because you don't want to
But the question is whom to?

Always the unchosen

You are a giver who
sometimes gives its own
piece of heart when needed.
But when you were empty
distributing
You didn't even receive a
vestige of it.

Always the unchosen

I think i was happiest when I
was with you,
i found myself laughing so
loud at the lame joke you
cracked,
for some reason you were
my escape from everything
that has hurt me and i never
wondered where to run
when the one you run to,
breaks you.

Always the unchosen

After all this,
now you've learnt to handle
heartbreaks on your own,
you have become a lot stronger
than you used to be.

Always the unchosen

Did you thank the Strom for making you realise that you are so strong to handle powerful wind trying to push you away while you stood firmed.
Some devastations of your life are reminders for you that you are strong.

Always the unchosen

I kept you in a way people
keep diamonds,
Locked in my diary,
Secured in my heart,
Far from every eye hidden in
the core of my art.

Always the unchosen

The more
love i poured
in you, the
more
poisonous
you became
to me.

Every song i listen to reminds me a piece of you.

Always the unchosen

Have you ever wondered
the number of times I've
written texts but
couldn't gather courage
to send them to you.

Always the unchosen

They said stay busy to feel nothing,
But even when I'm in the kitchen preparing dinner a part of me wishes i could serve you with my hands,
When I'm at the office I wish you too worked here so I can stare at you all the time,
When I'm using my phone i wish I could text you more,
Even when I'm achieving the thing I've waited 10 years for, i wish you were sitting in front and clapping out loud for me.
How can I feel nothing about you, when everything I do leads me to you.

Always the unchosen

And i craved you a little more every
time I absorb the wind.

Always the unchosen

You were like
the sunsets of
my life
beautifully
changing
colours every
time you were
about to leave.

Always the unchosen

Once you've been hurt from a place
you'll no longer find peace in them.

Always the unchosen

Being exhausted
doesn't mean you
aren't strong enough
to handle it,
sometimes even a star
too, is tired to shine.

If my mind was a place it would
be surrounded by moments
spent with you.

Always the unchosen

I don't care if somebody else owns
your heart, I'm grateful you own every
piece of me.
the beauty of one sided love.

The beauty of
remembering the
fragrance you felt 5 years
ago, it's something that
never makes you feel
alone you always sense
they are with you even if
the distance between you
is miles apart.

Always the unchosen

He said you chose the wrong guy for yourself
while tears slipped from his eyes,
My hands begged to wipe his tears and tell him
fate held it not me.
*It wasn't my decision to love you, it was the
wind knowing its path.*

Always the unchosen

After all,
The way people talk to you tells what
they think about you.

Always the unchosen

I love the familiarity of long conversations,
it always fixes a broken part of you, the
laughs and lame jokes make you forget
your current situation when you were
unable to shut your brain off.

Always the unchosen

A bird without wings,
sleep without dreams,
And humans without purpose,
Is existing but truly not living.

Always the unchosen

And why did I always relate broken poetry and not love once, why did it always feel like they wrote this for me, they wrote this about me. This makes sense that lately I've been through so much and never realised that life is being so harsh to me.

Always the unchosen

Looking back at my life and realising
I've always been left out almost in
every stage of my life,
Whether it was childhood games,
collage friendships, workplace
discussions or even family gatherings.
It always made me question my worth
in the world.

Always the unchosen

But those who never received love are
the ones to love the most,
Just like you.

Always the unchosen

And how do I expect that what's coming
is better than what has passed, when
life continuously gave every thing I
begged not to receive.
And after everything I've been through
at least I learnt, to never expect things
even when you see it coming to you, it
could leave by touching you.

Always the unchosen

No one really talks about the unanswered texts occupying your mind heart and the whole you. You just keep on being haunted by the reply you'd receive, as if the words could break you before they are even spoken.

Always the unchosen

Maybe I was a lot to handle but never a lot to lose.

Always the unchosen

I was the friend who left,
when the Storm was destroying you.
but you never knew I was handling a
hurricane that once held,
trying to shatter me into tiny
fragments unable to be fixed.

Always the unchosen

It could be people we spend 10years
with and still find hard to explain
ourselves or,
It could be people we spend 10 days
and don't even need words to explain
what we find hard to say.

Always the unchosen

The older you get the more you realise nobody ever kept you before themselves. "They were available for you when they had free time, but they never freed their time to be available for you."

Always the unchosen

Oh to have a guy who never writes about anything
but when it comes to me he owns a diary which
screams about me.
Oh to be loved by the guy.

Always the unchosen

It's hard to find people who notice your silence, especially for me because I never found one.
I never knew how it feels to be pampered just because I haven't spoken anything for a while.

Always the unchosen

The hardest thing is to let go of your favourite moments to turn into memories.

Maybe the chapter of
your life you're going
to walk-in, is the life
changing one.
Maybe in this one
you're going to find
the one you lost.

Always the unchosen

The act of waiting,
Waiting till?
As long as
I breathe—I endure—I exist, even when
it hurts to do so.

Always the unchosen

Should I be
grateful or
regretful for
still being in
love with those
eyes which
gifted me tears.

Always the unchosen

The beauty of your scars can never be described.

Always the unchosen

And the
value of me
in your life is
just like the
moon in
daylight.

Always the unchosen

The wilted
flower in my
favourite
book was a
lot more
precious than
a bouquet.

Always the unchosen

For as long as my heart remembers you,
I'll admire the way you left too.

Always the unchosen

You are present here even after you leave,
Just like the echoes of loss remain.

Always the unchosen

Sometimes
the light
gives you
Chaos while
the darkness
gives you
peace.

Always the unchosen

Indeed, i believe everything happens
for a reason,
But i still can't figure out what was the
point of making me fall in love with
you then marrying the other person.
What was the reason behind this?

I miss when I used to be excited for
my birthday, The countdown starts
from a month ago, and the wishes I
used to write on the paper, I miss the
purity of happiness i had in me.
i miss the kid in me.

Always the unchosen

The moments I've spent with you are filled with emotions and love, I'm unable to find in you now.

Always the unchosen

I've heard so much that no one can love you in the purest way, As your grandparents would. Unlucky I couldn't experience that either.

Unluckily,
The person who is supposed to love you the most is the person who hurts you the most.

And it was my fault for not being prepared
for the absence I'm going to feel,
before getting attached to you.

Always the unchosen

I don't know how do I get in the same
place again,
after running for so long,
Same pain after moving on.

Always the unchosen

What haunts you the most,
Horror movies or wild animals?
- Echoes of him leaving.

Always the unchosen

What do you want??? He yelled.

She mumbled ,
Just important to you,
As important as your morning tea.
Just precious to you,
As precious as the Locket your mom
gave to you.
Just being captured by you,
As you capture every sunset.
Just being able to own your mind,
As your T20 matches own your mind.
Just being your favourite,
As your favourite childhood ben -10
watch.
Just being loved by you,
The way you love your cigarettes.

Sometimes I ask him so many questions just
to hear that possessiveness he has for me
out but the reply I get is totally opposite.
It's not that I ask you so many questions
without any reason
I love when you get jealous or possessive
about me
It makes me feel wanted.

No one will read, no eyes will see, this page belongs your heart to be free.

write down to make your heart free.

About the Author

Amina has been passionate about poetry since childhood, often scribbling verses on the back pages of school books. Writing has always been a way to express deep emotions and be heard, transforming thoughts into art. With a lifelong dream of publishing a poetry book, Amina now shares her words with the world, hoping to inspire and connect with readers through the power of poetry.

www.ingramcontent.com/pod-product-compliance
Ingram Content Group UK Ltd.
Pitfield, Milton Keynes, MK11 3LW, UK
UKHW062256290726
14090UKWH00017B/715